My Grandma

By Julie Haydon

Photographs by Lyz Turner-Clark

Contents

My Painting of Grandma

This morning,
Grandma came to my house.
I painted a picture of her.

I got my brush and paints ready.
Then, I put paper on my easel.

Grandma sat in front of me.

First, I put pink paint on my brush.
I painted Grandma's head and neck,
and her nose and ears.

Then, I painted her short brown hair.
I dipped my brush
in the brown paint again,
and I painted Grandma's eyes.

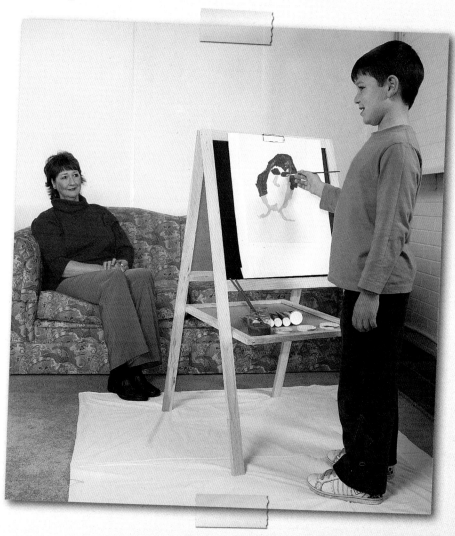

Grandma smiled,
so I painted her with a big red smile.

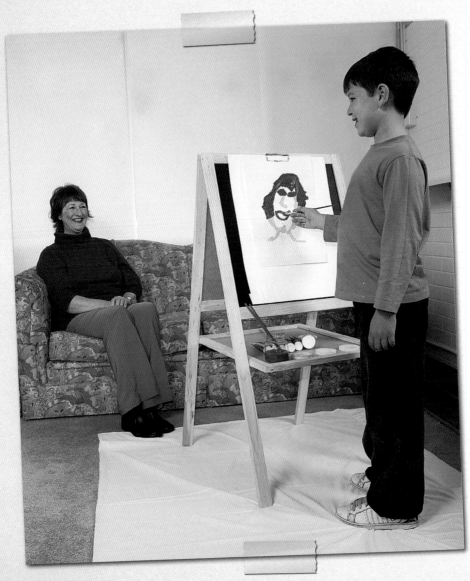

Grandma was wearing tiny gold earrings.
I painted two small dots of yellow paint
for her earrings.

Grandma looked at my painting
when it was finished.
She liked it very much.

I wrote my name on my painting
and let it dry.
Then, Grandma put the painting
on the fridge for everyone to see.

My painting of Grandma was just perfect.

Grandma

My Grandma is old.
She has some wrinkles around her eyes.
Grandma's eyes are brown
and her hair is brown, too.
Grandma always wears small earrings.

Grandma has three children
and six grandchildren.
She likes to play games
with her grandchildren.
She likes to cook with her grandchildren, too.
Grandma is a good cook.

Grandma has a little dog called Pluto.
She takes Pluto to the park every day.

Grandma has a little garden.
She grows vegetables and flowers
in her garden.
Sometimes, Grandma cuts
some of the flowers.
She puts them in a vase in her house.

Grandma likes to read.
She gets books from the library every week.

Sometimes, Grandma reads to me.
Grandma is a good reader.
She acts out the story when she reads.

Grandma takes me home from school
every Monday.

I love my Grandma
and she loves me.